D0169717

# OPEN MY EYES

*A Story of God's Mercy Revealed*

By

Kathleen M. Wabick

# OPEN MY EYES

ISBN # 1-932433-83-X

*Diary, St. Maria Faustina Kowalska, Divine Mercy in My Soul*
© 1987 Congregation of Marians of the Immaculate Conception, Stockbridge, MA 01263 www.marian.org . Used with permission.

Scripture texts in this work are taken from the Douay-Rheims Bible.

Cover photo:  Bernadette Andrzejewski, age 13

For information on how you can obtain additional copies of this book, please email: treasuresofgrace@roadrunner.com or visit our website at www.treasuresofgracellc.com

Printed in the United States of America by
Signature Book Printing, Inc.
www.sbpbooks.com

# *Acknowledgments*

First and foremost, I want to thank Jesus and His Blessed Mother for making this book a reality. They have blessed me with many caring people who have helped with this great task.

My husband, John, for his total support and for believing in me from the very beginning. I could not have completed this task without his help. I love you!

My children, Jason, Jamie and Jeremy, who are my treasures in life and have shown their love in so many ways.

My granddaughter, Joscelyn, whose love of Jesus and Mary has taught me the meaning of unconditional love.

My grandson, Baby Jude, as God prepares to bring him into our world.

My heavenly babies who supported me with their powerful intercessory prayers as they remain in the presence of God.

Bobbie and Nathan, for their encouragement and love.

Fran Campbell, for her tireless dedication and perseverance as she worked on editing the manuscript and for her tremendous moral support. Her efforts brought out far more in my writing than I ever imagined.

Mary Jo Weiss, for her advice, encouragement and spiritual support through prayer and also for the countless hours spent on editing the manuscript.

Marcia McCarthy, for her help with the great task of editing. I marvel at her strength and wisdom as well as her tremendous faith in God.

Anne Downey, for all of her guidance through this project and for her help in editing the manuscript. Her prayers lifted my spirit in ways known only to God.

Carol Lang, for her help in editing the manuscript and her quick response to my many questions.

Rev. Msgr. Richard Nugent, Rev. Jacek Mazur, Rev. Paul Keeling and Rev. Dan Fawls for their spiritual support and guidance along my journey of faith.

My brother Ted, my sister Barbara and all who were in the room the night we were blessed with hearing the Truth. May we never forget that we were witnesses of God's love and mercy.

My Godmother Aunt Dorothy, who has shown me so much love.

Ann Sullivan and Andrea Long, my long distance friends who were always a phone call away. They listened so patiently and offered sound Christian advice.

Cathy Kaiser, from Kaiser Design Studio, for her help in designing the cover of this book; Phil Nanzetta, from Signature

Printing who was so pleasant to work with; Mimi Romaniak, from Stockbridge, MA, whose kindness was such a joy!

Sharon Wicks, Ann Grisanti, Barbara Vullo, Terry Coughlin and Pat Weinreich, who provided me with the necessary prayer support.

Duffy O'Connor, whose interest in the book has kept me on God's path.

To anyone I fell short of mentioning…I thank you.

*Thaddeus and Bernadette Kalota*

This book is dedicated to my parents,
Thaddeus and Bernadette Kalota,
And
Consecrated to the Holy Trinity
In the Name of God the Father
Through our Merciful Jesus
By the power of the Holy Spirit.

At the beginning of my religious life, suffering and adversities frightened and disheartened me. So I prayed continuously, asking Jesus to strengthen me and to grant me the power of His Holy Spirit that I might carry out His holy will in all things, because from the beginning I have been aware of my weakness. I know very well what I am of myself, because for this purpose Jesus has opened the eyes of my soul...

~ Diary of St. Faustina, 56 ~

# Table of Contents

*The Kalota Family*

# *Preface*

My mother's death had a profound influence on me, and her visions of heaven at the time of her death changed my life forever. For years I asked God why He chose my mother. Why was she blessed to share with us a glimpse of heaven? I began to seek God for answers.

What I have discovered is that my mother was simply called upon to be an instrument for God's greater glory. She was a mere vessel, a humble person who God utilized at the time of her death, to draw aside the veil of heaven. This unveiling would be the beginning of a long journey for me. It has opened my eyes to see God in His mercy and love.

It is only through the grace of God that I was able to write this book. God desired that this story be told and so in complete submission to His will, I began this great task.

This story is about an ordinary woman who prayed every day, went to church on Sunday and observed all the teachings of her Faith. When people hear the story of my mother's visions of heaven, they ask me if she was extremely religious.

"She must have been special for God to bless her in this way," they say.

My mother was a simple, ordinary woman. Her faith was important and she taught her children to respect the

Catholic Faith. She did have a devotion to the Blessed Mother and prayed the rosary, but she was just an average person who God chose to deliver a powerful message.

My mother was a witness to the realism of heaven. It is a beautiful place prepared for us by our merciful God who loves us unconditionally. Moreover, it is a place that, at the time of our death, we will hopefully yearn for; a place where we will again greet loved ones who have gone before us and a place we will call our eternal home with God the Father, Son and Holy Spirit.

We will not be afraid, for Jesus promises that we will never be alone on this journey home. My mother was living proof of this. He remained with her, as well as everyone who was in her room the night she died.

This story is truly a miracle in itself. It never ceases to amaze me every time I take myself back to that night in October of 1998. Or should I say, GOD never ceases to amaze me! He is the reason we were granted this miracle of seeing a glimpse of heaven, and it is through His grace that this testimony is written.

May this story, through the mercy of God, bring an innumerable amount of souls back to Jesus and His Blessed Mother.

# *Foreword*

The reader of this beautiful story of a unique mother will discover the grace-filled ways of God. As we live our normal day, we may not have any suspicion of God's presence; yet He speaks to us and directs us without our being aware of Him. He is our daily Presence, and in this story, He rewards this mother for her life of suffering as she begins to leave for her eternal home.

Bernadette Kalota (Andrzejewski) lived a full life, yet most of her years were lived in extreme pain. She accepted her physical suffering and, with her husband Thaddeus, raised a loving family who were present to her needs. Physical pain followed Bernadette throughout her life, even to the moments prior to her death.

Her French name-sake, St. Bernadette Soubirous, to whom our Lady came in apparition eighteen times in 1858, lived a similar life of suffering in her last years of life. On one occasion, one of her superiors visited her during her sick confinement. She said, "What are you doing there in bed, you lazy little thing?" Bernadette responded, "I am doing my job." And "what is your job?", she responded. Bernadette said, "being ill!" (St. Bernadette, Trochu, p. 352)

Perhaps some neighbor or friend might have said the same of Bernadette Kalota as well. But read the story sometime of St. Bernadette and then read this story, and you will discover that you cannot tell a book by its cover. This Bernadette was older than the saint of Lourdes, but like her name-sake, lived a humble life of sanctity that only God could see and reward.

Her daughter, Kathleen Wabick, a wife and mother, was present with the entire family at the time of her mother's death and reports in detail the marvel of God's mercy. Her mother's life of penance and suffering came to a beautiful and grace-filled moment, which will amaze the reader.

We may think that God is not paying attention to our daily prayer and work offered to Him, but in time, God responds in a way that will surprise us. Suddenly, we realize that every thing we did for God and neighbor has its reward. And He will bless your children and their children for many generations. God cannot be outdone in generosity.

Now take a moment and enjoy this book. You will be amazed by the Mercy of God!

Rev. Msgr. Richard Nugent
St. Bernadette Church
Orchard Park, New York

*Bernadette Andrzejewski*

# *Her Death Brought Life*

Where was I spiritually at the time of my mother's death? How is it possible that the loss of a parent could bring about new beginnings in one's own faith and a new life centered in Christ? How could God use a simple, ordinary woman at the time of her passing to manifest His great mercy? Why, before she spoke of her visions, had she told us to get paper and a pen and write it all down? These are some of the questions I have pondered in my heart in the years following my mother's death.

God *can* and *will* use us in ways we never thought were possible because He is so merciful. We have to be open to hear Him speak. Our hearts should be ready, waiting for Him to enter, and in our readiness, we should be completely prepared to answer Him with, "Yes Lord, Thy will be done!"

My mother's astounding visions of heaven at the time of her death had a major impact on my life. They were a seed God had planted which would take many years of searching, deep within my soul, before they were cultivated. Once enriched, it gave me a greater appreciation for my Catholic faith; I grew more and more in love with Jesus truly present in the Eucharist, really yearning to receive Him often into my heart. I discovered that I, like many, was a sinner who needed to be healed by the One True Healer. Yes, I went to Sunday Mass, but I would soon realize that I did not have a personal relationship with Jesus Christ, the One Who died on the cross for me, the One Who was patiently waiting to reveal His Divine Love. It took many years immersed in prayer before I came to understand His purpose for me in this life.

I can still vividly remember that cold October day in 1998 as if it were yesterday, the day I made a distraught phone call to my friend Kathy, telling her of my unwillingness to accept my mother's grave illness. I was not ready to let go of the woman who gave me life, who nurtured me and cared for me. I was simply not ready, and I knew it. Can we ever be ready to witness the death of a parent or loved one? Even if we prayed and asked God for the grace to get through this most difficult time in our life, could we ever really be ready?

Kathy knew of a treasure that would bring many graces to my dying mother and she was about to share with me a remarkable devotion, one that would explode into a great mystery. This incomprehensible mystery, called the Chaplet of Divine Mercy, became for me a devotion that I came to know and love with all the fervor deep within my heart and with the utmost passion in my soul. Moreover, for me, it became a way of life.

As I sat at my mother's bedside, I held in my hands a new rosary I had just purchased the week before. My mother told me how much she admired it and relished the fact that I was showing an interest in praying the rosary, this powerful devotion she had long treasured. Needless to say, I never thought one week later I would be praying on that same rosary, imploring God's mercy for my mother through the powerful prayer of the Chaplet of Divine Mercy.

What would arise from this simple yet extremely powerful prayer would bring about many changes in my life, give me a new restored faith in God and bring me closer to Jesus and His Blessed Mother.

*Open my eyes, O Merciful God,*
*And let me see with the eyes of Jesus.*

*Today let me hear Your heavenly Words,*
*For I need Your guidance now more than ever.*

*Witnessing the death of a loved one is never easy,*
*But the presence of Your Divine Love can ease my pain*
*and relieve some of my misery.*

*Give me the gift of understanding*
*that nothing can happen to me,*
*You have not already willed.*

*Heavenly Father, refresh me with Your gift of peace.*

*O whisper to my soul, my sweet Jesus of Mercy.*

*The Candy Store*

# 2 *A Life of Suffering*

My mother experienced great suffering during her entire life. People who knew her would say to me, "I have never known your mother to *not suffer*." Through the years, I would come to know that her suffering was truly blessed by God in ways I could not even imagine.

## *Her Suffering as a Child*

My mother, Bernadette Andrzejewski, was born on November 27, 1921. She was raised above a candy store and was the second youngest of eleven children.

She knew suffering at a tender young age, enduring the pains of Juvenile Rheumatoid Arthritis. She told me numerous

*Bernadette Andrzejewski*
*8th Grade Graduation*

times how her swollen knees throbbed with pain while she scrubbed the kitchen floor of her parents' home. Silently, she withstood her discomfort when no one else knew she was suffering. Despite the affliction that was imposed upon her frail little body, she was expected to share in the household duties.

When my mother was just thirteen years old, her own mother died of cancer, leaving her father with the sole responsibility of raising several young children. Older siblings helped in raising the younger children but, in spite of this, she lived an ordinary happy life filled with many good times and laughter.

Graduating from eighth grade, my mother was forced to cease her formal education to devote time to the candy store, which eventually became a restaurant in the town of Cheektowaga, New York. The entire family contributed to the prosperity of the restaurant, making it a "local favorite" in our town.

In the summer of 1945, she married my father, Thaddeus Kalota, and together they had three children; my brother Thaddeus Jr., my sister Barbara and myself being the youngest.

From time to time, I reflected on my mother's life, contemplating the suffering she experienced, especially as a young child, and how she silently endured it all. Yes, she was afflicted with excruciating pain throughout her lifetime. Had she known the value of her suffering? Would she ever come to know what a treasure she truly possessed?

Perhaps, in the last hours of her life, she learned the value of her sufferings, as she tenderly kissed a crucifix that was held to her lips. It may have been an outward sign to us that our mother took up her cross and followed Jesus.

My mother's suffering extended into her adult years. Rheumatoid Arthritis remained throughout her lifetime causing an extreme amount of pain.

## My Father's Cancer

In November of 1963, at the young age of 42, my father received some devastating news. He had been diagnosed with a life threatening form of throat cancer.

The disfiguring surgery he must undergo to save his life, in itself, was a great cross for him *and* my mother to sustain. In fact, the removal of half of his tongue, teeth and jawbone forced him to once again learn how to speak and eat. In the beginning, his food had to be pureed and fed through a tube leading to his stomach. My mother placed her health concerns aside for now; my father needed all the help she could possibly give.

After his surgery, my father communicated to us by writing his thoughts on a small chalkboard. As time went on, doctors told my mother that my father must begin to *speak*. My father rejected this thought, for he knew it would be a struggle and he did not want to embrace it.

"Ted, it's time to learn to speak and we will be taking the chalkboard away," my mother instructed.

"I WILL NOT SPEAK," he wrote, striking the board with a tiny piece of chalk and underlining his words to express his discontentment.

"You will speak, and it will begin now," were my mother's stern words to him.

Stern...this was a disposition she knew well. She was the ideal person to help my father through this ordeal. Her ironhanded personality was the support my father needed. What seemed at times to be "cruel" or "ungentle" efforts on my mother's part, was the one thing that brought her husband back to a somewhat normal lifestyle.

With immense fortitude, my mother continued to aid him through these most difficult days. There she stood, keeping a watchful eye in all his countless frustrations. The man she loved was experiencing immense pain and unjust humiliation. He balked at facing people in public, and rightfully so, because of the

*My dad before his cancer surgery in 1963*

stares and strange looks from inquisitive people who wondered what marred the features of such a handsome, young man.

My father was angry, irritated and often offended by people who did not know any better. Indeed, my mother "bore her cross" a little differently now, since suffering manifests itself in many ways. My father was unable to work for a considerable length of time. Money became sparse, requiring my mother to work longer hours at the family restaurant. For all of us, it became a life of sacrifice. We learned that money does not bring happiness and gained sight of the fact that family takes care of each other, in good times *and* in bad. Blessings came from the pleasure and enjoyment of the simple things in life.

Furthermore, my father survived his bout with cancer and, after sometime, was able to return to his place of employment.

## Infectious Hepatitis

At the age of 53, several months before my wedding day, my mother was afflicted with infectious hepatitis. In order for her to survive she was placed on a lifetime of medications, most of which depleted her bones of the necessary calcium her delicate body needed. For her, this was be the beginning of yet another very difficult time in her life, an even heavier cross for her to embrace as she encountered the aftermath of a damaged liver.

She began to experience severe bone loss due to osteoporosis, and several falls landed her in the emergency room with several broken bones. A simple sneeze fractured her ribs, leaving her in tremendous pain. The basic chore of getting in and out of bed was next to impossible, making a hospital bed a necessity in her home. As time went on she used a walker to prevent future falls. Moreover, she eventually needed a wheelchair to lessen the pain of moving her legs.

It was August of 1989, twenty-six years after his first bout with cancer, that my father was diagnosed with yet another form of cancer. After the diagnosis, he remained with us for only a few short weeks before Jesus called him home. There was my mother at the bedside of her dying husband, watching him experience an extremely painful death. Her strength made a lasting impression on us all.

"Ted, it's ok to go now; your mother is waiting for you," she told him over and over as she placed cold washcloths on his feverish head.

This was my first personal involvement with death. For me, it came as somewhat of a shock. The screams and moans coming from my father, the thrashing of his cancer-filled body, were something I could not bear. Still, my mother remained at my father's side until God took him to his eternal reward.


## First Gastro Intestinal Bleed

Several years after my father's death, my mother's health took another major turn for the worse. She began experiencing piercing abdominal pains. Tests revealed she had *Esophageal Varices,* or swollen veins in the esophagus, resulting from the hepatitis. Her doctors explained to us the dangers stemming from this life threatening disease. At any time she could have a serious massive hemorrhage which would suddenly and very quickly end her life.

One day while doing the laundry, my sister noticed bloodstains on my mother's clothes and pillowcase. Questioning her about the stains, my mother was quick to respond with, "It's not blood, and if it is, I don't know where it came from." We knew my mother all too well and were certain she was concealing something from us.

The bloodstains became more numerous and we convinced her it was time to call the doctor. Thankfully she agreed and the next day she had surgery to repair the bleeding veins in her esophagus.

## *Visit by Her Guardian Angel*

As we all know, our Guardian Angels are powerful friends given to us by God to accompany us on our earthly journey. In the book of Exodus our Lord told Moses that He would send an angel to guard him. In the Acts of the Apostles, St. Peter is freed from prison through the help of an angel.

God blessed my mother with an extraordinary gift, a vision of her own Guardian Angel. One evening, a slight wind in her bedroom woke her from a sound sleep. She saw an angel who spoke not a word, only gazed so lovingly at my mother. The presence of the angel brought tremendous peace and tranquility to a suffering soul. Little did we know that through this angelic visit, God blessed my mother with courage and strength to withstand the stormy days that lay ahead.

When my mother described this visit by an angel, my sister Barbara and I began to ask many questions. What did the angel look like and what was she wearing? Did the angel speak to you?

My mother's continuous response was, "All I can say is this; there was peace all around me. Peace filled my room and surrounded my bed. I just felt so much peace."

So I began to contemplate this sense of peace that came over my mother through the grace of an angel. Peace...harmony, calmness, serenity, tranquility and contentment; her angel brought all this and more to someone who desperately needed to feel God's presence and His love. My mother soon experienced great tribulations. Her guardian angel came to deliver many treasures of grace from a merciful God.

## Second Gastro Intestinal Bleed

One year went by and it seemed like my mother's health had stabilized. This soon changed, for she endured more physical pain and suffering from a second gastro intestinal bleed.

I will never forget that warm, sunny day in the summer of 1994, when I was enjoying a pleasant round of golf with some friends. I was coming down the eighteenth fairway when, at a distance, I noticed my husband sitting in a golf cart.

"There must be an emergency with one of our children," I cried out as I ran towards him.

"It's your Mom," he said, "and it does not look good. She has been rushed to the hospital by ambulance."

John gave me the few details he knew as we raced to the hospital. When we arrived, my brother and sister were seated in the waiting room. They told me that my mother was bleeding profusely from the mouth, and paramedics said it was possible she would not survive. I saw my mother for a brief moment; her face looked so pale and lifeless. This woman, who was always so strong, now looked exhausted and exceedingly weak.

We quickly kissed her cheek as she was whisked away for more surgery to repair the ruptured varices. Could she possibly survive the surgery in such a weakened state?

God blessed her with a wonderful and amazingly talented doctor. He worked endlessly to stop the bleeding in her esophagus. As time went by, we were given the news. My mother was stabilized; she had survived a massive gastro intestinal bleed. The doctor managed, *this time*, to control the bleeding.


## Third Gastro Intestinal Bleed

Several years had passed and we felt God blessed my mother in so many ways. She held her own as far as the varices were concerned. Her arthritis and bone loss continued to deteriorate, but at least they did not appear to be life threatening.

By this time, she was almost totally confined to her wheelchair. The stairway to her apartment was now an obstacle and we needed to find a new place for her to live. Temporarily, she moved in with my brother Ted, while we searched for a handicapped accessible apartment.

One night my sister-in-law, Maureen, was awakened to a loud, knocking sound. It was my mother, pounding on the bathroom walls. Waking up my brother, they ran downstairs to find her profusely hemorrhaging into the bathroom trashcan. Time would be of the essence in order for my mother to once again survive. She needed help and she needed it fast. She needed her "angel of peace" to attentively remain at her side.

By the time the paramedics arrived, my mother had lost an enormous amount of blood. We were told she might not survive the transport to the hospital so we prepared ourselves for the worst.

It was hard to see my mother suffer as much as she did during these unfortunate hemorrhages. We learned that God was teaching us to trust in Him, for only He was in control of her destiny.

To our astonishment, her doctor again managed to control the bleeding in her esophagus. God granted us another miracle; my mother's small frail body again survived a very serious gastro intestinal bleed.

How was it possible that someone this fragile and weak could survive? Why had God allowed her suffering to continue to escalate in strength? Why had He allowed her to survive when all odds were against her?

My mother's suffering had a purpose and we were soon presented with the most precious gift and reassurance that our God is full of love and mercy.

*Bernadette Andrzejewski*
*First Holy Communion*

*Thaddeus Kalota*
*First Holy Communion*

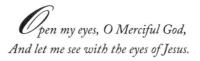

*Open my eyes, O Merciful God,*
*And let me see with the eyes of Jesus.*

*As I meditate on the Passion of Your Son, I begin to realize*
*that no one can suffer as inexhaustibly as Jesus.*

*He so willingly accepted great torments upon His Sacred Body,*
*Because of the sins of the world for all of time.*

*To endure all the scourges,*
*All the beatings, to be spat upon and laughed at,*
*To be stripped of all His clothes;*
*Purely because of love He stretched out His arms*
*and was brutally nailed to a Cross.*

*This is how He welcomes us… with open arms.*
*This is how the Triumphant One invites us*
*to unite our sufferings with His.*

*O Heavenly Father, this takes my breath away!*

*Jesus was stripped of everything He owned,*
*But His most precious possession they could not take away from Him,*
*His Blessed Mother Mary.*

*He hung from the Cross for three long grueling hours,*
*And humbly died for all to see.*

*Jesus took upon all of this because of our sins,*
*Out of pure Love and Divine Mercy.*

*May I know God that You are with me*
*in my joys and in my sorrows, in my comforts and in my pains.*

*I need only to call upon You and Your cohort of heavenly angels,*
*Then peace will encompass my soul.*

*May I know that my own sufferings are never in vain,*
*For You have truly shown me the humble pathway to heaven*
*through Your Son Jesus Christ.*

*God, I need you beside me on this journey of faith,*
*I am unable to walk it alone.*

*O whisper to my soul, my sweet Jesus of Mercy.*

# 3 *Our Heavenly Babies*

**M**y sister Barbara and I share a common bond. We both were given the honor of having powerful intercessors in heaven...our dearly beloved babies who were taken home to Jesus. I say *honored* because I feel that if God takes a precious child from us, He must have a divine purpose for what seems the worst tragedy any parent could ever experience.

My sister's baby, Jessica, was borne to heaven on October 22, 1977. This was our family's first experience with the loss of a child. I grieved for my sister and tried to be strong for her. But how could I help her when I did not fully understand the quiet sufferings deep inside her motherly heart? This soon changed, for I also experienced the loss of a child. We grieved for each other in ways we both could understand.

Our first child, baby John, entered heaven on April 26, 1978. I was 20 weeks pregnant when I felt something was going terribly wrong. As a precaution, my obstetrician asked me to meet him in the emergency room for a brief physical exam upon which he discovered I had an incompetent cervix. The baby was starting to slip through the opening in my uterus and an emergency procedure must be performed in order for the baby to survive. Gently pushing the baby back up into the uterus, the doctor closed my cervix with a strong suture. Within twenty-four hours I went into labor and we realized the surgery was not a success. The suture was removed so I could have a vaginal delivery and we prayed that our baby was strong enough to survive. Several hours later, the labor pains came to a complete halt and we were given the devastating news.

"Why can I no longer hear my baby's heartbeat on the monitor?" I asked my assigned nurse.

I will never forget the disheartened look on her face as we exchanged glances. No words were needed...I knew my baby had died in my womb. Labor was induced and I soon gave birth to my lifeless baby.

No one could prepare my husband and me for what we were about to experience. We would not hear our baby's first cry, nor would we see him wiggle his little toes or move his tiny fingers. With my husband John at my side, our baby was delivered in my hospital bed. Our sweet, tiny, beautiful child of God was so quickly taken away from us.

Our second loss was an early miscarriage, giving us two children who live in God's presence. Our first grandchild, baby Jesse, is also among our heavenly babies. I have come to understand that our babies are powerful "prayer warriors," and it is through their heavenly prayers that God grants many graces.

At first I questioned God and asked Him why He needed our children in heaven. Could we not, beyond the question of a doubt, need and love them more? For reasons beyond my human understanding, my children needed to return to their heavenly kingdom and I had to learn that God would never do anything that would be harmful to my soul. God eventually brought good out of something that went so terribly wrong.

When we were growing up, there was a picture in our home. It was Jesus knocking on a door…a door which had no handle. Jesus could not open the door because it must be opened from the other side. When Jesus knocks, He patiently waits for our answer.

During this time of great tribulation in my life, Jesus was knocking at the door of my heart. He wanted me to know that He was near and He would take something *bad* and make it *good*. I did not open the door when Jesus knocked. But God in His mercy did not give up on me. He used my mother's death to open my eyes to His goodness.

John and I were soon blessed with three healthy children…Jason Andrew, Jamie Kathleen and Jeremy John. I wept when I heard their first cries. I savored the moment when I could pass my fingers through theirs and kiss their soft angelic faces. My children are my "treasures" because God taught me a lesson on the value of life. Life is a gift and it should never be taken for granted since it is so precious in God's eyes.

## My Mother's Vision of the Babies

After my mother's survival of her third gastro intestinal bleed, she moved into a handicapped accessible apartment. She lived there for only a year and a half when she became totally bedridden because of her osteoporosis. Simple movements in bed broke tiny bones in her frail body. Tending to her every need, we tried our best to keep her comfortable. The entire family helped to make my mother's last months as relaxed and calm as possible.

One day while changing her clothes, she pleaded with me to stop because the pain was too intense. The simple rotation of her body caused tremendous pain. What my mother needed to survive, we could no longer provide. Our best was no longer good enough.

The decision was made to seek the help of professionals and place my mother in a skilled nursing facility. It broke my heart to realize that we could no longer give her the quality care she needed at home, but her well-being was to be of the utmost importance. She needed twenty-four hour professional care.

A few weeks after her admittance into the nursing facility, my mother told my sister and me that she could see our heavenly babies. She recognized that they were in the room with us.

"Jessica is here," she said.

"And Kathy, your two baby boys are here also. I can see them. They remain at your shoulders, following you everywhere around the room. Climb into my bed and get close to me so I can touch them because they will not leave you."

Honoring her wishes, we climbed into her bed. My sister and I managed to get as close to my mother as we possibly could. Unable to hold back the tears, we wept as my mother spoke about the babies God took home to heaven so many years ago. She revealed to us again that they remained with us as we moved about the room. These words brought my sister and me tremendous consolation. It was a blessing sent to us from God.

Through my tears I responded, "Mom, tell us more about them. What do they look like?"

"They have blond hair," she revealed to us, "and beautiful blue eyes. They are real and I can touch them," she said as she stretched out her arm towards us.

*Touch them?* Does this mean she can see them in bodily form? Is this possible?

Scripture tells us that all things are possible through God. Yes, I thought to myself, *everything* is possible for God. Absolutely everything.

## *Approaching Death*

After a few days, my mother's abdomen became very distended, hardened and extremely uncomfortable. Upon her physical examination, we were given the news and our worst fears became a reality. She was in complete liver failure.

Previously, I had a long discussion with her about her health. She told me her wishes if she could no longer make the necessary decisions on her own. It was time to honor those wishes.

We met in a small room in the nursing home, my brother, my sister, the doctor and me. Staring into the doctor's eyes I asked him, "Is there *anything* you can do to save my mother?" The doctor replied, "She is in complete liver failure. I am sorry; there really is nothing more we can do for her."

She rejected any food that was offered but willingly accepted small sips of water. At this time she received the Sacrament of the Anointing of the Sick from a priest.

As my mother approached her death, it was God's grace that brought us the greatest gift of all…an amazing glimpse of heaven.

*Open my eyes, O Merciful God,*
*And let me see with the eyes of Jesus.*

*In my most difficult moments, let me think only*
*of the love and peace of heaven.*

*Where there is sickness no more,*
*Nor tears, nor pain,*
*Nor sorrow of losing a loved one.*

*Only gladness and joy await us there,*
*Along with all the angels and saints.*

*For this is what Jesus has promised to those*
*who take up their cross and follow Him.*

*I pray for all the souls of my family members*
*who have gone before me.*

*May the warmth of God's love*
*shine forever on their face.*

*I joyously await that day*
*when I will see them again in glory,*
*To praise our God together for all eternity!*

*Remain with me Lord, as my ship sails towards Your Love.*

*O whisper to my soul, my sweet Jesus of Mercy.*

*Bernadette Andrzejewski*

# 4

# The Visions:
# A Gift of God's
# Mercy

## The Beginning of God's Grace

My mother's death was drawing near and I knew the time was approaching when I would have to say my final good-bye. All the years of tending to her needs would soon come to a complete halt. How would I accept this drastic change in my life?

I sat silently, looking at her lying there so peacefully. I decided to open the devotional booklet to the Chaplet of Divine Mercy, given to me by a friend. Just then my sister-in-law, Maureen, walked into the room. We agreed that together we would pray for my mother.

Knowing very little about this prayer, I reached for my rosary and began to follow the prayers that Jesus gave to St. Faustina Kowalska so many years ago. For me, this is where it all began… the beginning of my journey towards Jesus.

Finishing the prayers, we closed our booklets. We discussed how it seemed God was bringing about an awareness of this wonderful devotion to His mercy. I had so much more to learn about the graces that come from reciting it and that God does hear and answer all our petitions, *if it is according to His will.*

## *Private Revelation*

What I am about to tell you is a private revelation. Yes, I know private revelation is not needed for our salvation. Jesus Christ willingly died for our sins out of pure love for you and for me. Private revelation does not teach us any new facts about our faith, but it can give us a better appreciation of it. For me, it provided a greater understanding of the Catholic faith and the awareness of the many graces we can obtain through the sacraments. It also enhanced my desire to read Sacred Scripture.

My mother had beautiful visions of heaven at the time of her death and she was able to reveal them to us. This wonderful *gift of God's mercy* was a grace that had a remarkable purpose.

For eight long years I have discerned and prayed about these visions. Along the way I have seen God begin to work in peoples lives, especially my own, for His greater glory. I began to realize it was God's will that this story be written and shared with others.

## *She Opened Her Eyes*

It was the next day after we prayed the Chaplet of Divine Mercy at my mother's bedside that she began to lapse into a semicomatose state. She remained in this state for almost twelve hours when, to our amazement, the next day at 12 a.m. she opened her eyes and asked us to sit her up in bed. We honored her wishes. She requested that we get a paper and a pen.

"Mom, you can hardly sit up in bed; I don't think you will be able to write," I replied.

"I am not going to write, one of you will. Write down everything that I say," she said. We looked at each other in astonishment.

*Write everything down…*is she actually going to begin to speak to us? How is this possible?


## *Her Glimpse of Heaven*

Her mouth was extremely dry as she began to share her visions with us. We took moistened swabs and gently wiped her parched lips so she could speak more easily. She glanced over at her granddaughter who held the paper and pen; she wanted to make sure we were following her instructions by *writing everything down.*

"I see the Father," she said.

"Mom, are you telling us that you see Dad?" we responded.

"No", she said, "I see the Father."

"You see *your* father?" we asked again.

Her response was slow as she proclaimed, "*I said…I see… THE FATHER!*"

I remember sitting next to her bed wondering how this could be. Was my mother really seeing God? The room became silent as we anxiously awaited her next comment. She *was* seeing our Heavenly Father and in a desperate attempt to portray Him, she was searching for celestial words. There were none.

Portraying the magnificence of God is simply beyond words.

Suddenly, Jesus appeared to her and it was obvious that He was visible in all His splendor and glory! He was in her

*Thaddeus Kalota*
*1941*

*Antoni and Wladyslawa Kalota*
*~my father's parents~*
With
*Thaddeus Kalota and Bernadette Andrzejewski*

room and she could clearly see Him. In a blissful conversation with Him, my mother was reciting the words, "Yes, I will, yes…" over and over. This clearly was her "fiat" to Jesus, for whatever He was asking of her and whatever He was revealing to her, she was in full acceptance of His Divine Will.

What was Jesus desiring of her? We wondered if our Lord was asking her if she loved Him? Would she want to be with Him forever in Eternity? Was she aware that He died for her sins? My mother directed her confirming words to Jesus, for He was a welcomed Guest in her soul. With a meek and gentle voice, she repeated her words of acceptance, "Yes, I will…"

Certainly, we wanted to know what Jesus looked like, so we proceeded to ask her to describe Him. Her only response was, "He is so beautiful…so beautiful and so handsome!" My mother was witnessing a beauty beyond anything on earth, a beauty known only to those privileged to see Him. How can anyone put something so mystical into words?

Her description of Jesus was brief but certainly majestic for we knew there was so much more to His beauty than we could ever humanly imagine. The radiance of our Lord must be *inexpressible*…it must be *unspeakable*.

Our Blessed Mother came to bestow special graces upon my mother, as she does to all who faithfully meditate on the Life, Death and Resurrection of her Son Jesus, through the recitation of the rosary.

My mother softly spoke, "I see Our Lady."

I immediately responded, "Mom, you see our Blessed Mother!"

"Yes, and she is so beautiful!" she expressed as she gently swayed her head back and forth in amazement. "She is just so beautiful!"

My mother's lips were extremely dry and she signaled us to moisten them; it was obvious she had more to reveal.

I see three Persons, but They are One," she said.

My niece immediately responded, "She sees the Trinity!"

31

*Bernadette Andrzejewski*

I sat next to my mother's bedside in total wonder and, staring into her eyes, I sensed an all-embracing peace in her soul. God in His Divinity was permitting my mother to see a great Mystery...the mystery of the Trinity. This vision presented us with a greater awareness of the true mystery of our Faith.

My mother clearly understood that no words could ever fully express what she was experiencing. For the sole purpose of presenting us with the most important gift of all, she was going to attempt the unthinkable. Through her amazing strength, she would find the words to describe her glimpse of heaven, accomplishing this only through the grace of God.

## *The Gateway*

"I see a gateway that I will be going through," she revealed to us.

"There is a word above this gate...*Laude*. I can see the letters," she said.

Pronouncing each letter slowly, she made sure we totally understood that she was seeing them above the gate upon which she would be entering.

"L-A-U-D-E," she recited to us.

"Mom, this is a Latin word you are seeing," my brother remarked. "It means glory and praise".

"Yes, I know," she said as she shook her head in approval.

*She knew this?* How could she? She had only graduated from eighth grade and Latin was a language she never studied. There was no way that she could spell this word, or, better yet, know the meaning of it...*unless* she was indeed seeing it; *unless* God was truly revealing its meaning to her!

I was so intrigued with what she was telling us that I asked her, "Tell us again, Mom. Where do you see this word?"

"Above the gate that I will be entering," she replied.

"Can you say the word again?" I asked.

*"Laude,"* she again perfectly pronounced.

My mother told us she would be passing through this gateway, but not at this specific point in time. It would be only in God's time that she would be allowed to enter. God wanted my mother to reveal more of the wonderful place He had prepared for her.

Through this gateway she told us that many souls were praising God, although they were praising Him in a language she could not understand. She heard heavenly chanting along with beautiful angelic music.

"Can you hear that?" she asked.

"Hear what, Mom?" we replied.

"Can you hear that beautiful music? And the beautiful voices, can you hear them singing?" she questioned us.

"We cannot hear what you are hearing," we responded.

"Shhh…can you hear them singing?" she asked again.

The entire room remained completely still. Our earthly ears could not hear these angelic voices coming from heaven. This gift from God was meant only for my mother, but we shared in her joy that these extraordinary sounds were bringing her great peace.

At this point a nurse entered the room and quietly whispered that she would like to stand in the back of the room to observe. She said she would not disturb us, only that she was intrigued with the visions God was revealing to us through my mother. We welcomed our considerate guest.

My mother then pleaded with her grandchildren to lift her body and "push her through the gate." This entrance into heaven, this gateway, was something that was so tangible to her. She was facing God's kingdom like a little child standing outside a candy store, with her face pressed up against the window. With her eyes wide open, beholding a glimpse of heaven, my mother so desperately wanted to be with our Lord.

She began to again have a conversation with someone.

"Yes…O.K…. yes…" she repeated several times.

Family members who had gone before her had appeared to her. She called them all by name.

"They are telling me it is not time to go through the gate," she solemnly said.

My mother glanced at me and said, "Kathy, do you remember when I told you I was afraid to die?"

"Yes, Mom, I do," I quickly replied.

How could I forget? Several weeks ago she told me that death frightened her and she did not want to die. Her children and grandchildren meant the world to her and she did not want to leave them.

"Well, now I am not afraid to die," she declared. "I want to go through the gate, but they keep telling me it is not time!"

What could I say? How could I respond to this? I was certainly happy that she was no longer afraid to die, but in my selfishness, I did not want to part with her. I replied with a smile and told her to rest awhile.

My mother had a glimpse of heaven, a beautiful, peaceful place where we will one day experience the great magnificence of God. How could anyone who encounters heaven want anything else?

## *The White Robe*

My mother asked the grandchildren to remove her clothing. She revealed that she would not need her clothes because Jesus had a white robe for her to wear.

"They have a long white robe for me," she told us.

"They will be placing it on me when I go through the gate!"

We realized this was the robe she would wear upon her entry into heaven.

*The white robe?* What was this meaning of the white robe? At this point in my life it had no significant meaning. None at all…but after my mother's death it would bring me great consolation. I would soon learn of God's omnipotent mercy.

## Her Passing

After three long hours of conversing with my mother we all agreed she should try to get some rest. By now it was 3 a.m. My mother softly spoke these words,

"They are telling me it is time for me to go through the gate."

"I love you," she repeated over and over as she kissed a crucifix that my brother touched to her lips. "I love you…I love you."

We knew these words were directed to us, but we also knew she was telling Jesus how much she loved Him. By kissing the crucifix on my brother's rosary, she was able to demonstrate this without the use of words. Her eyes, which were once wide open with the excitement of seeing her eternal reward, were now gently closing.

Her breathing became shallow. Her face appeared angelic. She was leaving her earthly body peacefully. For one hour more we prayed. We cried. Embracing each other, we observed our mother depart from us.

Then with one deep unexpected breath…her soul went to Jesus.

*Open my eyes, O Merciful God,*
*And let me see with the eyes of Jesus.*

*How often I am too busy to pray;*
*My days seem sometimes full of my duties in life.*

*And yet, You always remain with me,*
*For You are my strength and my hope.*

*In You, I confide all my joys and sorrows,*
*In You, I share all the desires of my heart.*

*So I just want to tell You,*
*From the bottom of my heart that*
*I love You!*

*When I enter the darkness of night,*
*I know I can call on You and*
*You will deliver me.*

*Be merciful to me Jesus, when You call me home.*
*May You always know how much I love You*
*and desire to be embraced by Your merciful arms.*

*O whisper to my soul, my sweet Jesus of Mercy.*

*Thaddeus and Bernadette*

*Bernadette with her father,
Michael Andrzejewski, and her
future father in law,
Antoni Kalota*

# 5 Realization of God's Will

## Many Weeks Later

A few weeks passed after my mother's death and I knew in my heart there had to be more to this testimony of faith. Why did she tell us to *write everything down?* I took the notes of my mother's vision of heaven to my parish priest. He told me that he was unable to help, but I needed spiritual guidance and I was not going to give up.

I decided to pay a visit to another local parish, St. Bernadette Church in Orchard Park, New York. My mother's name was Bernadette and for some reason I felt a strong connection with this church. Could God have been pointing me in this direction? I called the rectory and asked to speak to the pastor.

"Father Nugent," he cheerfully answered. I explained to him that he did not know me but that my mother had visions of heaven when she was dying and I needed advise from a priest. He told me that he would be willing to speak to me and asked if I could come right over. I gratefully accepted the offer.

Monsignor Richard Nugent welcomed me into his office. When I entered, I saw a humble man sitting behind a desk. He stood up and with a genuine smile on his face, reached across the desk to shake my hand saying,

"And your name is?"

"Kathy," I said, "Kathy Wabick."

"Please, have a seat Kathy," he directed me.

He wanted to know more about me, about my family, my husband and children. He showed an interest in someone he met only minutes ago. I was very impressed with this meek and mild priest. He recognized the importance of guiding me in this matter and was willing to direct me according to the teachings of the Catholic Faith.

We discussed my mother's visions and I gave him a brief explanation about how she instructed us to write everything down on paper.

Monsignor Nugent looked at me and said, "God has a purpose in allowing your mother to share her visions of heaven."

"Can you tell me what that might be?" I asked.

"I don't know," Monsignor said. "But I think you should pray and ask God to reveal it to you. This may take some time…six months, a year or maybe two years; but everything is in God's time. It is important that you pray and tell God that you are seeking His help. Then, when God reveals His will, you will feel a sense of great peace," he added.

Monsignor Nugent did not know me, yet he took the time to speak with me. That day, I saw Jesus in this very holy priest. By demonstrating his true concern, Monsignor Nugent was teaching me a lesson on "loving thy neighbor" and living a life in Christ.

## Learning How to Pray

So now I had some sense of direction...*pray and ask God to reveal His will for you.* I thought to myself, how am I going to do this? I realized that I did not know how to pray so I began the only way I knew, by praying the rosary that had been taught to me so many years ago.

Our Blessed Mother Mary is the perfect model of prayer, and she knew something was missing from my prayer life. She felt certain that I needed to learn more about her Son, Jesus Christ and that I needed to know Him in a very personal way. Through the guidance of the Blessed Mother, and by the power of the Holy Spirit, I became more deeply centered in the life of Christ.

I also realized that I needed to return to the Sacrament of Reconciliation and seek God's forgiveness for my sins. Not only did I need to seek the One True God, but I also had to eliminate the false gods in my life. I had to remove everything that would hinder my relationship with Him. This would take great effort on my part and I had to cooperate with His good grace. At this point in time, I deeply and humbly submitted myself to do God's will, whatever it may be, as an expression of my love for Him. I begged Him to help me be a better Christian and to seek Him in all things.

I started asking myself many questions. If someone asked me about my Catholic Faith, could I explain it to them? Did I know what was taking place during the Mass when I worshipped every Sunday?

When I began searching for answers to my mother's visions, I realized there was a good deal about my faith that I *did not* know. I had a long way to go; I had so much more to learn.

God in His mercy knew this and He was patient with me. I realized I had to start my climb up the very steep hill in order that God might enlighten my soul.

# The True Presence of Jesus in the Eucharist

I began to experience a greater awareness of Jesus truly present in the Eucharist. Although this great Mystery was explained to me long ago, my eyes were not open to accept the Truth. I have since learned that the Holy Eucharist is not a thing, but a Person. It is not a symbol. The Eucharist is truly the Body and Blood of our Divine Savior, Jesus Christ!

One and a half years after my mother's death, I slowly began to understand some of God's will. By the grace of God, my friend Kathy and I started a Perpetual Eucharistic Adoration program in our parish. Eucharistic Adoration is where we are willing to spend a quiet holy hour of prayer with Jesus in His Eucharistic Presence. For me, spending quiet time in the presence of God brought about a personal dialogue of love with Him. It was in these quiet moments of adoration that He whispered to my soul.

God taught me how to strengthen my prayer life by acquiring different forms of prayer, especially prayers of petition, intercession, praise and thanksgiving. Through the reading of Sacred Scripture accompanied by prayer, I felt my own journey in faith begin to grow.

I began thirsting for good religious books that could help me grow in the knowledge of God. One day, I began reading the diary of St. Maria Faustina Kowalska in the adoration chapel and found it to be very inspiring. Jesus appeared to St. Faustina in 1935 and dictated to her the Chaplet of Divine Mercy. I cultivated an interest in this humble saint and was eager to learn more about the devotion to the Divine Mercy, the prayer I recited at the bedside of my dying mother.

Thoughts of forming a Marian prayer group entered my mind, so I approached several women who had been coming regularly into the chapel and asked them if they would be interested in praying the rosary together. We began meeting one day a week to pray in adoration before the Blessed Sacrament.

*Michael and Helen Andrzejewski*
*25th Wedding Anniversary*

I shared the story of my mother's visions and told them about the Chaplet of Divine Mercy. We began to recite this prayer along with the Holy Rosary, and soon God blessed our friendship. A bond was forming between us, and I knew in my heart that God had placed us together for a reason.

A slight sense of peace came over me. Eucharistic Adoration was up and running in our church and our Marian prayer group was offering powerful intercessory prayers to our Lord. I say a slight sense because I knew God had additional plans for me. More of His will was yet to be revealed.

Once again I met with Monsignor Nugent and we discussed all that had taken place since our first visit. I told him how I felt that God had more to ask of me. Monsignor directed me again to an even stronger prayer life.

"Keep praying," he told me, "and God will take care of the rest. If there is more, He will let you know. Keep seeking His direction."

I started spending more time with Jesus in Adoration and began praying, "Lord, I only want what is pleasing to You. Please show me the way!"

Three years after my mother's death and through divine grace, I came to eventually see God's plan more clearly in my life.

## *The Phone Call*

One early morning the phone rang. It was a good friend of mine, Fran Campbell, and there was a sense of urgency in her voice.

"Kathy, it's Fran," she said as she proceeded to tell me that God had placed something on her heart.

"We have to go to Rochester as soon as possible."

"Rochester?" I replied.

"Yes, and the sooner the better! There is a young man who is dying, and God wants us to pray with him and his family. This feeling just came over me and I know God wants us to do this, Kathy! It's important that we pray the Chaplet of Divine Mercy at his bedside. If anyone from our Marian prayer group wants to go, we can ride in our van and my husband Tom will drive," she said.

I agreed with Fran. If she felt this strongly, then we must make this lengthy trip. My thoughts immediately went back to the time I prayed this powerful prayer at my dying mother's bedside. God bestowed so many graces upon my mother, and I knew He would confer them upon this man as well.

Through the diary of St. Faustina, I often contemplated the greatness of God's love and began to learn how to pray for His mercy. But now, above all, I needed to begin imitating it. It was now time to show mercy to others.

## *Our First Act of Mercy*

A call was placed to the family, asking them if we could come to pray. They graciously accepted the offer, so six of us piled into Tom's van and journeyed to Rochester, New York.

When we arrived, we found the man's mother at his bedside. I looked into her eyes and knew she had a common bond with our Blessed Mother. She was witnessing the death of her son.

We greeted her with the assurance that God is all merciful and revealed to her the many graces her son would receive through this very beautiful prayer of the Chaplet of Divine Mercy. Together we trusted that God, who is rich in mercy, would shower many blessings upon this family.

## The Realization

As our prayers unfolded, I knew God was showering His mercy upon this man's soul and I suddenly realized that I was to begin to take this prayer, the Chaplet of Divine Mercy, to the bedside of other people who were sick and dying. God allowed my mother to share her vision of heaven in order that I might come to know of His mercy. Her beautiful death sparked my interest in this devotion and I came to understand that my mission of spreading God's mercy was only beginning. Finally, peace filled my soul and I knew in my heart this must be part of God's plan.

During our journey home, I shared this idea with my friends. I asked them if they would be willing to join me in this great mission of mercy. Everyone agreed, and we knew if this was truly God's will, then He would certainly direct us. I began to pray for courage and asked God to help me, for I knew I could not do this alone. In my humanity I was frail and weak, but in Jesus I would be made strong.

In the weeks to follow, an ad was placed in our church bulletin and we started receiving calls to come and pray at the bedside of many people who were sick and dying. God blessed us with meeting brave and courageous souls who touched our lives in so many ways. We witnessed God's mercy in action.

I revisited Monsignor Nugent and shared the news of my realization of God's will. Because I was blessed to be guided by him, my entire family decided to become members of his parish. In August 2002, we became proud members of St. Bernadette Church.

# Great Graces

Jesus promised special graces when we pray the chaplet at the bedside of a dying person. St. Faustina tells us in her diary,

*"The following afternoon, when I entered the ward, I saw someone dying, and learned that the agony had started during the night. When I verified it – it had been at the time when I had been asked for prayer. And just then, I heard a voice in my soul:* **Say the chaplet which I taught you.** *I ran to fetch my rosary and knelt down by the dying person and, with all the ardor of my soul, I began to say the chaplet. Suddenly the dying person opened her eyes and looked at me; I had not managed to finish the entire chaplet when she died, with extraordinary peace..."* (Diary, 810)

The promises of Divine Mercy reveal how important each one of us is to God. When we pray the Chaplet of Divine Mercy, Jesus will grant us everything we ask for, *if it is according to God's will.* By exalting the mercy of God, which is love and compassion, we are therefore worshipping Him. God is Wisdom; God is Omnipotence; God is Love and God is Merciful.

Only when we get to heaven will we ever completely comprehend the magnificence of God's mercy. His mercy is endless. St. Faustina wrote this in her diary,

*"Praise the Lord, my soul, for everything, and glorify His mercy, for His goodness is without end. Everything will pass, but His mercy is without limit or end. And although evil will attain its measure, in mercy there is no measure."* (Diary, 423)

It is significant in this powerful devotion to trust in God and show love towards our neighbor. When there is a strong bond of trustfulness between us and God, and when we show love, even to our worst enemies, God will show us His mercy.

In essence, the Divine Mercy is so much more than a devotion...it becomes a way of life.

St. Faustina said it so perfectly...when love is put into action, it becomes mercy.

*Open my eyes, O Merciful God,*
*And let me see with the eyes of Jesus.*

*Help me to trust in Your mercy*
*when I bear heavy crosses in my life.*
*Let me feel Your presence in my soul, O God.*

*May I continue to seek Your will in all things;*
*For I only want to do what is pleasing to You.*

*And when I fall into sin and seek Your forgiveness;*
*Teach me to trust in Your endless mercy!*

*Above all, use me as a good instrument in Your hand;*
*Help me to show love and mercy to everyone*
*You have placed in my life.*

*O whisper to my soul, my sweet Jesus of Mercy.*

*St. Faustina's Baptismal Font*

*Holy Relics of St. Faustina*
*St. Casimirs's Church*

# 6 *Miracle of Mercy*

## *My Greatest Fear*

I have often contemplated what it would be like to visit my homeland, the country of Poland. I call it my homeland because this is where it all began for me, as both sets of my grandparents were born in this beautiful country. This has always been a passing thought, for my fear of flying would get in the way of pursuing my dream of one day making this wonderful pilgrimage.

After several years of praying the Chaplet of Divine Mercy at the bedside of the sick and dying, I developed an interest in a humble Polish nun, St. Maria Faustina Kowalska. I discovered more about her spirituality and her deep love for Jesus, but the greatest lesson I learned was how she surrendered herself to God and trusted in the fulfillment of His complete will.

The idea of visiting the Shrine of the Divine Mercy and St. Faustina's tomb in Cracow, Poland, often entered my mind, but in an instant, fear got the better of me and I realized that as beautiful as these thoughts may have seemed, they were just passing reflections.

I discovered in St. Faustina's diary that she experienced great afflictions in her lifetime. She reveals,

*"At the beginning of my religious life, suffering and adversities frightened and disheartened me. So I prayed continuously, asking Jesus to strengthen me and to grant me the power of His Holy Spirit that I might carry out His holy will in all things, because from the beginning I have been aware of my weakness." (Diary, 56)*

These inspiring words gave me hope. St. Faustina experienced fear amongst her greatest difficulties, and she turned to Jesus as her source of strength.

I admired this in her, this *attitude* of trust in the midst of her trials, and what evolved in me was a genuine desire to try to live by these virtues in order that I may begin to trust God in many aspects of my *own* life. My fear of flying was real and, in order for God to heal me, I had to make a drastic change in my attitude.

I began asking God for a healing of this fearfulness that had taken hold of me. I prayed believing that I would be healed, but it would be according to God's will and in God's time. Years came and went, and my fear of flying continued to be an obstacle that robbed me of many wonderful opportunities. But in my heart I knew for certain that God would show me His mercy. Then one day the invitation came…an opportunity to travel to Poland.

It started out as just an amusing conversation with a few of my friends but very quickly turned into a reality. Panic set in and I could not believe that I actually showed an interest in traveling across the ocean! What was I thinking? Was I absolutely out of my mind?

I knew what I was thinking. The thought of visiting St. Faustina's birthplace appealed to me; paying a visit to her final

*The Kowalski Family Home*

resting place at the Shrine of the Divine Mercy in Cracow was a desire God had placed on my heart.

How could I possibly find the strength and courage to make this journey? I uncovered the answer in the words...*Jesus, I trust in You!* These words appear at the bottom of the renowned image of the Divine Mercy that is based on a vision our Lord gave to St. Faustina.

I needed to open my heart to God and let His healing touch alleviate my worries and concerns. I needed to place my fear of flying in God's hands and *trust* that He would, or better yet, He *could* bring me the necessary peace of mind to make this pilgrimage. I knew it would take enormous courage to accomplish this great task, but could I really do it? Could I really trust that God in His mercy would help me?

Mary Jo, a good friend of mine, gave me some beneficial advice. She suggested that in order to overcome my fears, I should try to move *through them* and not run *away from them*. These words of wisdom offered me great strength. I immediately recognized them as a compelling message from God, for it was in these words that God was trying to show me His compassion and mercy.

I knew in my heart that I must walk towards my greatest fear. I must get on the plane and fly to Poland.


## *The Journey*

I opened my mailbox and there it was...my plane ticket to Poland. My hands trembled as I struggled to unseal the envelope. Gazing upon the itinerary, I kept saying over and over in my mind, *walk through this fear Kathy, and trust in God.*

The devotion to the Divine Mercy played an important role in the lives of the friends who joined me on this pilgrimage. Fr. Jacek Mazur was born in Poland and he graciously offered to be our tour guide. The enthusiasm was building as we finalized

*Inside the Kowalski Family Home*

all our plans to leave on September 1, 2006. I still harbored a tremendous fear of entering the aircraft that would fly me miles across the ocean. I tried to work on my attitude, trusting that God would embrace me with His mercy, but unexplainable fear darkened the excitement.

On August 10, several weeks before our trip, a massive mid-air terrorist plot was uncovered, which caused a major disruption in flights to and from Europe. My first notion was to cancel my airline reservation as quickly as possible. I thought to myself, "Lord, You are really testing me with this one! I am trying to place all my trust in You, but this one is taking me over the edge!"

If I was going to attempt to get on this plane and make this long pilgrimage, I needed some assistance. I contacted my doctor and he agreed to prescribe a mild sedative, which would help with my uneasiness. I was disappointed that I had to depend on this medication to help me with my phobia, but I kept praying that God would ease some of my fear and anxiety. I decided not to cancel the trip, and, beyond all doubt, I was pursuing my long journey to Poland.

September 1st was here before we knew it. Our flight was to depart from Buffalo, New York at 3 p.m. …the hour of God's mercy! As explained in St. Faustina's diary, the three o'clock hour is the hour of Jesus' death on the cross and the opening up of God's infinite mercy for all who call upon Him.

When we arrived at the airport, we discovered that a horrendous wind and rainstorm was quickly approaching, causing some travel delays. Fr. Jacek suggested we pray the Chaplet of Divine Mercy so we moved ourselves to a quiet place, asking God to please calm the storm so our plane could depart within a reasonable amount of time. After a two-hour delay, we boarded our plane to New York City. We made our connecting flight and by midnight were on our way to Warsaw, Poland.

Surprisingly, because the medication sedated me, I was able to sleep for six tranquil hours. When I woke up it was

*Window to room where St. Faustina died*
*October 5, 1938*

*Convent Chapel in Cracow, Poland*

evident that my long time dream would become a reality. The medication helped to calm my fears and I could feel the excitement develop as I began to contemplate our agenda for the next two weeks.

As the plane was descending into Poland, I asked God to bless my journey to this region that my ancestors called home, a place I thought I would never see with my own eyes.


## St. Faustina's Place of Birth

Our first day in Poland we toured Warsaw and visited the Motherhouse where St. Faustina first entered the convent of the Sisters of Our Lady of Mercy. The next day our plans were to visit St. Faustina's hometown and place of birth.

After a short journey by train and a hair-raising ride by taxi, we arrived at St. Casimir Church in Swinice Warckie, the place where St. Faustina was baptized, made her first confession, first Communion and obtained her initial calling to the consecrated life. Stepping out of the taxi, we felt blessed to be visitors in this small village. We glanced at our watches and we were amazed to see that the three o'clock hour was quickly approaching.

Upon entering the church, the sisters invited us to join them in the prayers for the three o'clock hour and the Chaplet of Divine Mercy. We felt God had blessed us with a wonderful gift…to recite the chaplet publicly for the first time in Poland, right in St. Faustina's hometown church!

When the sisters began reciting the prayers, I could not hold back the tears. As my fingers passed over each bead of my chaplet rosary, I thought of a young girl named Helena Kowalska (St. Faustina's birth name), who prayed in this same church so many years ago. I envisioned her to be a humble, holy child of God who piously said her prayers and longed for the religious life. I could not help but wonder if, as a small child, she

knew deep down in her soul one day she would accomplish great things for God.

After our prayers were finished, Fr. Jacek went to get permission to enter St. Faustina's home. We remained in our pews and prayed until he returned with the most wonderful news. Not only would we set foot in her house, but also we would be coming back to St. Casimir Church to celebrate Mass with Fr. Jacek as a concelebrant!

The Kowalski family's brick and limestone house was located two miles away from the church in a tiny Polish village called Glogowiec and consisted of only a few small rooms. We were told that when St. Faustina was a child, she used to move rapidly through the fields behind her home to get to her church. It was a shortcut she discovered that allowed her to spend more time in front of the tabernacle with Jesus.

When we entered the little cottage, it was noticeable that the Kowalski family lived a life dedicated to God. Religious pictures so beautifully decorated the walls, and the sparse furniture was evidence of their simplicity. We remained in total wonder and, out of respect for this great saint, we could hardly speak.

Fixing my eyes upon the faded wooden floor, I bent down to touch it. In my mind I imagined the many times her father paced this very floor as his wife gave birth to their children; I pondered the countless times her mother washed this very floor on her hands and knees. I came to realize that we visited firsthand, a place that could truly be called *a home blessed by God.*

Time was running short and we had to return to St. Casimir Church for Mass. As Father was in the sacristy preparing to concelebrate, we suddenly perceived what was about to take place. In this significant house of worship, through the priestly hands of our dear friend Fr. Jacek, we would be receiving Jesus in the Eucharist.

The meek and humble parishioners of this devout community, so proud of the accomplishments of their great saint, eagerly welcomed us with open arms as we celebrated Mass

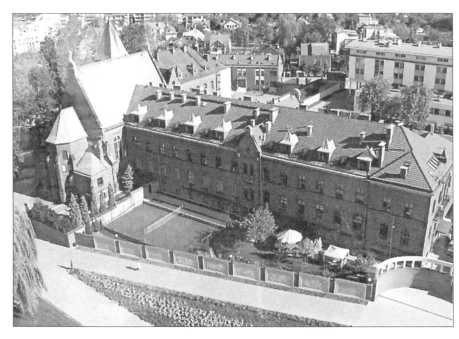

*St. Faustina's Convent in Cracow, Poland*

together. With language as our only barrier...we were all one with Christ.

## St. Faustina's Final Resting Place

Observing the beautiful countryside of Poland on the train to Cracow, I contemplated being in the presence of the saintly remains of St. Faustina. What would be my reaction as I came so near to her final resting place? She has been such a beautiful role model for me, particularly because of the attentive manner in which she displayed her love for others, her deep devotion and love of God and her willingness to trust in the rays of God's mercy.

As the train arrived in Cracow, our enthusiasm was growing. We unloaded our bags and quickly hailed a taxi. For me, the utmost significance of my pilgrimage was to finally visit the Shrine of the Divine Mercy and the tomb of St. Faustina. I was so excited and bubbling over with joy as we briefly checked into our rooms and headed for the convent chapel to pay homage to this great Apostle of Divine Mercy. This was, above all, the most soul-stirring moment of my religious journey.

Approaching the chapel, Fr. Jacek directed our attention to a beautiful window off to the right of the convent. Glancing upward, we observed that it was adorned with a multitude of lovely white flowers, cascading down over the windowsill. This was the room where on October 5, 1938, St. Faustina was called home to Jesus. In silence, we stood there for a moment, and with our eyes fixed on her window, we reflected upon this sacred day when Jesus mercifully embraced His "secretary of Divine Mercy."

Fr. Jacek, my friend Sharon Wicks and I then entered the chapel; a serene feeling came over me. We immediately knelt down and remained in prayer for a few moments. I silently prayed, "After all these years, St. Faustina, I can't believe I am finally here!"

I was so anxious to come close to her tomb. At the time of my mother's death, St. Faustina brought me knowledge of the mercy of God through the prayers of the Chaplet of Divine Mercy. Because of her trustfulness she gave her "fiat" to do God's will and served as a channel of His great mercy for all of humankind.

After a few minutes, I stood up to approach the altar. I genuflected to our Lord in the tabernacle and slowly moved toward the side altar. Above this altar hung the most beautiful miraculous image of the Divine Mercy. Below the image was the tomb containing the mortal remains of St. Maria Faustina.

Placing my knees upon the kneeler, I kissed her sacred relics which were encased in a beautiful reliquary near the altar rail. I lifted my head to venerate the image of the merciful Jesus and from the innermost dwelling of my heart I quietly prayed,

"Dear Merciful Jesus and St. Faustina...for a long time I have dreamed of this day; a day I thought would never come. Jesus, I come here in thanksgiving and offer everything to You. How can I ever thank You for all the blessings You have bestowed upon my family through the prayers of the Chaplet of Divine Mercy, above all, especially my mother at the time of her death? St. Faustina, you are an inspiration to me and I thank you for the many times you have interceded on my behalf..." and then I bowed my head and began to weep. My tears fell upon the glass encasing the holy relics of St. Faustina; I humbly wiped them away. At this precise moment my body began to quiver and something unexplainable happened to me.

I felt that I was being infused with some sort of grace, and yet I was totally unaware that through this grace, a transformation was taking place. God chose this specific moment to answer the desires of my heart, a moment I often longed for, a moment I knew would come...*in God's time.* Firm hope in God strengthened my trust, and in this trust God sent graces from His fountain of mercy. At the tomb of my beloved Saint Faustina, God granted me a miracle.

A hand softly touched my shoulder; it was my friend Sharon standing directly behind me. She also kneeled down to venerate the relics of St. Faustina and together we prayed a little while longer. For a moment, time seemed to stand still.

Leaving the chapel, we stood again beneath the window of the convent room where St. Faustina died. We embraced each other and together shed more tears of joy. I revealed to Sharon and Fr. Jacek that something had happened to me in the chapel near the tomb of St. Faustina. I shared with them my sense of being "infused" with some sort of grace and Fr. Jacek suggested that a healing might have taken place. Could I possibly have been healed from my fear of flying?

I tried to place my thoughts on the flight home. No anxiousness, no fear, only peacefulness filled my heart. Sharing my excitement with Fr. Jacek he quickly responded, "Let's wait and see." He knew me all too well. If this were truly a miracle, time would soon tell.

We spent several more days at the Shrine of the Divine Mercy in Cracow. Each morning began with the church bells ringing at 6:00 a.m., Mass at 6:30 a.m. and morning prayer with the sisters afterwards; it was truly heaven on earth.

During the next week we traveled throughout Poland, and each day in my thoughts, I placed myself on the return flight home; still no fear. Again, I shared these feelings with Fr. Jacek and this time he told me, "Kathy, try not to take the medication on the trip home. See if you can get on the plane without it."

I smiled and knew in my heart that God had healed me.


## *Saying Farewell, But Never Good-Bye*

After fourteen days of beautiful sunshine (thank you, Blessed Mother), it was time to say farewell to this marvelous country of Poland. So many captivating memories had been forever sealed upon my heart through these miles traveled with special friends and numerous acquaintances that were gathered along the way.

No medication was necessary on my return flight home because my fear of flying was no longer a hindrance in my life. As my husband John says, "Kathy now has her wings!" With my merciful Jesus as my only source of strength, I joyfully boarded the plane home in order that I may continue to seek the will of God and help spread His Divine Mercy.

While gazing out the window as the plane departed, I felt truly blessed to take with me a lasting remembrance of this beautiful country of Poland.

"I take these memories with me when I leave, but my heart I leave at the tomb of St. Faustina, for it was through her intercession that God healed me. My dear Poland, I must now say farewell, but I will never say goodbye. For if it is God's will, I shall return. My beloved St. Faustina, until we meet in heaven, farewell...*do widzenia!*."

*Open my eyes, O Merciful God,*
*And let me see with the eyes of Jesus.*

*When my trust in You begins to go astray,*
*Let me be mindful of Your faithful servant,*
*St. Maria Faustina Kowalska.*

*In her humility, she displayed a spirit of trust,*
*For You, Almighty God, was all she*
*needed in her life.*

*She totally surrendered to Your will,*
*And with tremendous faith and hope*
*trusted in Your goodness.*

*May the words Jesus I trust in You,*
*Be those I fall back on when the road to heaven*
*gets difficult to travel.*

*And when blessings come my way,*
*May I always know You are the Source of everything*
*good in my life.*

*O whisper to my soul, my sweet Jesus of Mercy.*

*Bernadette Kalota (Andrzejewski)*
*1994*

 *The Light of Life*

My mother's visions at the time of her death opened my eyes to many things. I discovered that my journey in faith is an opportunity for me to one day be united with God forever in Eternity. Sometimes I will fall, but with God as my strength I will pick myself up and continue to walk with Him. Consequently, the road can become rough and difficult to travel; the crosses we carry can become heavy. It is in times like these that God has shown me that I am nothing without Him.

Everything my mother was able to tell us points to a gracious God who, out of complete love for us, gives us only what is beneficial to our soul...He gives us the gift of His Divine Mercy. Our omnipotent God will remove the darkness and provide us with the light of life.

# The Mystery of Suffering

Several years after the death of my mother, I was eager to learn something from her sufferings. I used to think she was a recipient of bad genetics, but oh, how wrong I was! Instead, I discovered that she was blessed by God. My mother was truly a suffering soul.

St. Faustina tells us in her diary,

*"Oh, if only the suffering soul knew how it is loved by God, it would die of joy and excess of happiness! Some day, we will know the value of suffering, but then we will no longer be able to suffer. The present moment is ours."* (Diary, 963)

There were so many times that my brother, sister and I witnessed tremendous suffering in our mother's life. When I think back on some of those times, I remember her always holding a rosary in her hand. Silently, she may have been uniting her sufferings with those of Jesus on the cross, asking Him to take her sufferings and offer them to God the Father. She may have suffered for many souls, maybe even her own. Only God knows what good came from her many afflictions.

I realized that God uses suffering as a tool in order that we may become more intimate with Him. Through suffering, our faith will grow like never before.

St. Faustina shares this about her feelings of suffering,

*"Suffering is the greatest treasure on earth; it purifies the soul. In suffering, we learn who our true friend is."* (Diary, 342)

At the end of my mother's life, it was comforting to know that Jesus remained at her side. Jesus told St. Faustina that He would always remain with her, especially in her darkest hour. On one occasion He told her,

***"My daughter, suffering will be a sign to you that I am with you."*** (Diary, 669)

St. Faustina again reveals,

> *"...I would not know how to suffer without You, O Christ.*
> *Of myself I would not be able to brave adversities. Alone, I would not*
> *have the courage to drink from Your cup; but You, Lord, are always*
> *with me, and You lead me along mysterious paths."* (Diary, 1654)

The mystery of suffering makes sense when we fix our eyes on the Crucified Jesus. It is by His wounds that we have been healed. He is the One True Healer.


## *The White Robe*

During my mother's visions, she told us she would be wearing a long white robe as she entered through the gate. What was the meaning of this white robe?

After her death, I wanted to learn more about Sacred Scripture, so I joined a bible study group in my parish and together we studied the Book of Revelation. God used His Word to explain to me the meaning of the white robe.

> *"After this, I saw a great multitude, which no man could*
> *number, of all nations and tribes and peoples and tongues,*
> *standing before the throne and in sight of the Lamb, clothed*
> *with white robes, and palms in their hands.*
>
> *And one of the ancients answered and said to me: These*
> *that are clothed in white robes, who are they? And whence*
> *came they? And I said to him: My Lord, thou knowest. And*
> *he said to me: These are they who are come out of great*
> *tribulation and have washed their robes and have made*
> *them white in the blood of the Lamb.*
>
> *Therefore, they are before the throne of God: and they serve*
> *him day and night in his temple. And he that sitteth on the*
> *throne shall dwell over them. They shall no more hunger nor*
> *thirst: neither shall the sun fall on them, nor any heat. For the*
> *Lamb, which is in the midst of the throne, shall rule them and*

*shall lead them to the fountains of the waters of life: and God
shall wipe away all tears from their eyes.* (Rev. 7:9,13-17)

I learned that the people whom John sees in the Book of
Revelation are the *redeemed* and they formed a "great multitude"
which no one could count. They have endured a time of *great
suffering*, their robes were made white by the "Blood of the
Lamb." For this reason they stand before God and worship Him
day and night.

Yes, my mother survived a time of great suffering. I
trust that through the many trials she endured, her robe was
made white by the Blood of the Lamb, Jesus Christ.


## Laude

The Latin word *laude,* meaning glory and praise,
appeared above the entrance of the gateway in my mother's
vision. She was very clear in her spelling and pronunciation of
this word and what amazed us the most was her ability to know
its meaning. At the time of her death, my mother's knowledge
of the word *laude* was truly a powerful message from God.

I turned to Scripture to help in my realization of the
importance of glorifying God. I found my answer in the Book of
Psalms. In the Psalms I discovered hymns of praise and worship,
songs of thanksgiving to God, as well as prayers for help and
protection. Most importantly, when I read the Book of Psalms I
discovered God's infinite mercy.

I sometimes meditate on the beauty of this heavenly place
in my mother's vision, the abode of all the choirs of heavenly
angels and saints, glorifying and admiring God's goodness
unceasingly day and night. Above all, I remember how my mother
heard celestial singing accompanied by angelic voices and I think
to myself, yes, heaven is real. What a beautiful place this must be,
this Kingdom of Heaven, this mystical City of God!

## God's Small Vessels

I do believe that God used my mother, graced by these beautiful visions of heaven, to bless us with messages of His Divine Mercy. My whole family witnessed firsthand God's great mercy through her beautiful death. Even though she had amazing visions of heaven, we still offer Masses and pray for her soul.

Through my mother's death I have learned that God is full of compassion, love and mercy. I can only hope and pray that I was able to convey these same messages to you, for I am only one of the many small vessels used by God to help spread His mercy.

Heaven is real, and God wants all of us with Him in eternity. However scarlet our sins may be, He stands before us with open arms, waiting to grant us forgiveness.

May we all delight ourselves in the healing rays of God's omnipotent mercy!

*Open my eyes, O Merciful God,*
*And let me see with the eyes of Jesus.*

*May I always know that following You*
*will provide me with the light of life.*

*Through the many trials and sufferings that I endure,*
*I pray that my robe will be made clean by the Blood of the Lamb.*

*Forever may these words remain upon my lips,*
*Jesus, I Trust in You!*

*O whisper to my soul, my sweet Jesus of Mercy.*

*The Kowalski Family Well*

# *Afterword*

In order to live a meaningful life one must first understand the meaning of suffering. There are times in our lives when the song of Mary (the *Magnificat*) becomes our song,

"My soul doth magnify the Lord.
And my spirit hath rejoiced in God my Saviour.
Because he hath regarded the humility of his handmaid:
For behold from henceforth all generations shall call me blessed.
Because he that is mighty hath done great things to me:
And holy is his name.
And his mercy is from generation unto generations,
To them that fear him. (Lk 1: 46-50)

These moments remind us of how blessed we are as Christians, as followers of Christ. Living our lives in the state of grace, receiving the sacraments of the Church, we participate in the very own life of our God, taking into ourselves not only our Lord, but everything that He taught, lived for, stood for and died for. We testify that we are ready to carry on His mission in this world.

Our suffering has a great value in the eyes of God when we unite it with the suffering of our Savior Jesus Christ. In this way we participate in the salvation that Jesus brings. Faith and trust help us to conquer our worries and anxieties.

The life and suffering of Bernadette Kalota (Andrzejewski) revealed to us in this book is an example for us of how to accept our daily cross and bear it to the end with dignity of a child of God. The example of the lives of the saints, like Saint Faustina, tremendously helps us to achieve the goal of our earthly pilgrimage – eternal salvation.

Inspired by this book, may we always have in mind that this life on earth is only a journey, that we are but pilgrims in this world and that we are all called to spend eternity with our loving Father in heaven. One thing is for sure; we cannot be indifferent toward God's offer of mercy. God wants to see fruits in our lives. We have to act now! Now is the time of mercy!

Rev. Jacek P. Mazur
St. Teresa's R. C. Church
Niagara Falls, New York

# How to Recite the Chaplet of Divine Mercy

## (on ordinary rosary beads)

### Begin with:

Our Father..., Hail Mary..., I believe in God...

Our Father, Who art in heaven, hallowed be Thy name; Thy kingdom come; Thy will be done, on earth as it is in heaven. Give us this day our daily bread; and forgive us our trespasses as we forgive those who trespass against us; and lead us not into temptation, but deliver us from evil. Amen.

Hail Mary, full of grace. The Lord is with thee. Blessed art thou among women, and blessed is the fruit of thy womb, Jesus. Holy Mary, Mother of God, pray for us sinners, now and at the hour of our death. Amen.

I believe in God, the Father Almighty, Creator of heaven and earth. I believe in Jesus Christ, His only Son, our Lord. He was conceived by the power of the Holy Spirit, and born of the Virgin Mary. He suffered under Pontius Pilate, was crucified, died, and was buried. He descended to the dead. On the third day He rose again. He ascended into heaven, and is seated at the right hand of the Father. He will come again to judge the living and the dead. I believe in the Holy Spirit, the holy Catholic Church, the communion of saints, the forgiveness of sins, the resurrection of the  body, and the life everlasting. Amen.

## On the five large beads:

Eternal Father, I offer You the Body and Blood, Soul and Divinity
of Your dearly beloved Son, Our Lord Jesus Christ,
in atonement for our sins and those of the whole world.

## On the ten small beads:

For the sake of His sorrowful Passion, have mercy on us
and on the whole world.

## Conclude with: (after five decades)

Holy God, Holy Mighty One, Holy Immortal One,
have mercy on us and on the whole world. (3 times)

# The Five Forms of Devotion to the Divine Mercy

1. The Image of the Merciful Jesus
2. The Feast of Divine Mercy
3. The Chaplet of Divine Mercy
4. The Hour of Mercy
5. Spreading the Divine Mercy Devotion

**1.** <u>The Image of the Merciful Jesus</u> – On February 22, 1931 St. Faustina saw Jesus in her room in the convent. She recorded this in her diary…

*"In the evening, when I was in my cell, I saw the Lord Jesus clothed in a white garment. One hand was raised in the gesture of blessing, the other was touching the garment at the breast. From beneath the garment, slightly drawn aside at the breast, there were emanating two large rays, one red, the other pale. In silence I kept my gaze fixed on the Lord; my soul was struck with awe, but also with great joy. After a while, Jesus said to me,* **Paint an image according to the pattern you see, with the signature: Jesus, I trust in You. I desire that this image be venerated, first in your chapel, and then throughout the world.***"* (Diary, 47)

The two large rays in the image represent the blood and water which flowed from Jesus' pierced heart. Jesus explained, *"the pale ray stands for the Water which makes souls righteous. The red ray stands for the Blood which is the life of souls. These two rays issued forth from the very depths of My tender mercy when My agonized Heart was opened by a lance on the Cross."* (Dairy, 299)

When we gaze upon this image, we can see that it illustrates the great mercy of God. The words "Jesus, I Trust in You" appear at the bottom of the image. Jesus attached promises to the veneration of this image, when combined with deeds of mercy. He promises eternal salvation, great progress on the road to Christian perfection, the blessings of a happy death and all other graces we ask for. Just gazing upon the image can be a form of prayer but only if you practice faith and trust in God. It is Jesus Himself who distributes graces through this image.

**2.** <u>The Feast of Mercy</u> – this is celebrated on the first Sunday after Easter and is the highest among all the forms of the devotion to the Divine Mercy. There is a correlation between this day and the first Sunday after Easter. This is the octave of the Resurrection of our Lord. The Passion, Death and Resurrection of Jesus are the most profound unveiling of God's mercy, and this day is designated for the worship of His mercy.

Jesus attached great promises to his feast day when He told St. Faustina,

*"My daughter, tell the whole world about My inconceivable mercy. I desire that the Feast of Mercy be a refuge and shelter for all souls, and especially for poor sinners. On that day the very depths of My tender mercy are open. I pour out a whole ocean of graces upon those souls who approach the Fount of My Mercy. The soul that will go to Confession and receive Holy Communion shall obtain complete forgiveness of sins and punishment. On that day all the divine floodgates through which grace flow are open. Let no soul fear to draw near to Me, even though its sins be as scarlet. My mercy is so*

*great that no mind, be it of man or angel, will be able to fathom it throughout all eternity. Everything that exists has come forth from the very depths of My most tender mercy..."* (Diary, 699)

Jesus directed St. Faustina that on this day, the image of the Divine Mercy was to be solemnly blessed and displayed. He asks us to receive the Eucharist in the state of grace meaning, detached from all sin and He asks us to perform acts of mercy. On this day, Jesus desires to bestow many graces upon us. He grants us complete forgiveness of sins and punishment. There is no limit to God's mercy. In preparation for the Feast of Mercy, Jesus told St. Faustina to pray a novena which consisted of the recitation of the Chaplet of Divine Mercy for nine days beginning on Good Friday. Jesus said, " By this novena, I will grant every possible grace to souls." (Diary, 79)

3.     <u>The Chaplet of Divine Mercy</u> - Jesus dictated this prayer to St. Faustina on September 13-14, 1935. In this prayer we are offering to God the Father the Body and Blood, Soul and Divinity of Jesus Christ for the forgiveness of our sins and those of the whole world. When we pray the Chaplet of Divine Mercy, we are performing an act of mercy because we are imploring God's mercy for us and for the whole world. Jesus states that He will grant anything we ask of Him, *if it is according to His will.* Jesus will grant a happy death for those who pray the chaplet as well as to those for whom we pray.

Jesus told St. Faustina this about the chaplet,

*"Whoever will recite it will receive great mercy at the hour of death. Priests will recommend it to sinners as their last hope of salvation. Even if there were a sinner most hardened, if he were to recite this chaplet only once, he would receive grace from My infinite mercy. I desire that the whole world know My infinite mercy. I*

*desire to grant unimaginable graces to those souls who trust in My mercy.*" (Diary, 687)

**4.**      The Hour of Mercy - Jesus told St. Faustina He desires that the exact moment of His Death on the Cross be venerated every day. During this hour, Jesus asks us to meditate on His Passion and to beg for mercy for ourselves and the whole world. This precise moment (3 p.m.) all of our requests are to be directed to Jesus. Jesus told St. Faustina,

*"Try your best to make the Stations of the Cross in this hour, provided that your duties permit it; and if you are not able to make the Stations of the Cross, then at least step into the chapel for a moment and adore, in the Blessed Sacrament, My Heart, which is full of mercy; and should you be unable to step into the chapel, immerse yourself in prayer there where you happen to be, if only for a brief instant."* (Diary, 1572)

Jesus told St. Faustina that there were three necessary conditions for prayers during this hour:  the prayers are to be directed to Jesus, the prayers should be said at 3 o'clock in the afternoon and we are to reflect on Jesus' Passion. We are to pray this prayer with trust that God will answer our prayers, if it is according to His will.

*"In this hour,* Jesus says, *I will refuse nothing to the soul that makes a request of Me in virtue of My Passion"* (Diary, 1320)

**5.**      Spreading the Divine Mercy Devotion- Jesus encourages us to spread the Divine Mercy Devotion. Jesus told St. Faustina,

*"Souls who spread the honor of My mercy I shield through their entire lives as a tender mother her infant, and at the hour of death I will not be a Judge for them, but the Merciful Savior."* (Diary, 1075)

For those who spread this devotion, Jesus has promised motherly protection through out their entire lives and to show them His mercy at the hour of their death.

Jesus also said,

*"All those souls who will glorify My Mercy and spread its worship encouraging others to trust in My mercy, will not experience terror at the hour of death. My mercy will shield them in that final battle..."* (Diary, 1540)

# Ways to Perform Acts of Mercy

When we perform an act of mercy towards our neighbor, we are showing God how much we love Him. Jesus told St. Faustina,

*"I demand from you deeds of mercy, which are to arise out of love for Me. You are to show mercy to your neighbors always and everywhere. You must not shrink from this or try to excuse or absolve yourself from it. I am giving you three ways of exercising mercy toward your neighbor: the first – by deed, the second – by word, the third – by prayer. In these three degrees is contained the fullness of mercy, and it is an unquestionable proof of love for Me. By this means a soul glorifies and pays reverence to My mercy.* (Diary, 742)

Jesus revealed to St. Faustina three ways that we could perform works of mercy. The first is by deed, the second is by word, and the third is by prayer. If our time is limited and we cannot perform a deed of mercy, then we can say a kind word to someone who is in need or we can offer prayers for that person. Below is a list of ways we can perform works of mercy.

# Good Deeds:

1. Prayer
2. Fasting
3. Alms-giving

# Spiritual Works of Mercy:

1. Admonish sinners
2. Instruct the uninformed
3. Counsel the doubtful
4. Comfort the sorrowful
5. Be patient with those in error
6. Forgive offenses
7. Pray for the living and the dead

# Corporal Works of Mercy:

1. Feed the hungry
2. Give drink to the thirsty
3. Clothe the naked
4. Shelter the homeless
5. Comfort the imprisoned
6. Visit the sick
7. Bury the dead

# Prayers From the Diary Of St. Faustina

## O Mary, My Sweet Mother

*O* Mary, Immaculate Virgin,
Pure crystal for my heart,
You are my strength, O sturdy anchor!
You are the weak heart's shield and protection.

O Mary you are pure, of purity incomparable;
At once both Virgin and Mother,
You are beautiful as the sun, without blemish,
And your soul is beyond all comparison.

Your beauty has delighted the eye of the Thrice-Holy One.
He descended from heaven, leaving His eternal throne,
And took Body and Blood of your heart
And for nine months lay hidden in a Virgin's Heart.

O Mother, Virgin, purest of all lilies,
Your heart was Jesus' first tabernacle on earth.
Only because no humility was deeper than yours
Were you raised above the choirs of Angels  and above all saints.

O Mary, My sweet Mother,
I give you my soul, my body and my poor heart.
Be the guardian of my life,
Especially at the hour of death, in the final strife.
(Diary, 161)

# Prayer To Do God's Will

Eternal God, Goodness itself, whose mercy is
incomprehensible to every intellect, whether human or angelic,
help me, your feeble child, to do Your holy will as You make it
known to me. I desire nothing but to fulfill God's desires. Lord,
here are my soul and my body, my mind and my will, my heart
and all my love. Rule me according to Your eternal plans.
(Diary, 492)

# In Suffering

My Jesus, support me when difficult and stormy days come,
days of testing, days of ordeal, when suffering and fatigue begin
to oppress my body and my soul. Sustain me, Jesus, and give me
strength to bear suffering. Set a guard upon my lips that they
may address no word of complaint to creatures. Your most
merciful Heart is all my hope. I have nothing for my defense but
only Your mercy; in it lies all my trust. (Diary, 1065)

# For the Grace of a Happy Death

O merciful Jesus, stretched out on the cross, be mindful of the
hour of our death. O most merciful Heart of Jesus, opened with
a lance, shelter me at the last moment of my life. O Blood and
Water, which gushed forth from the heart of Jesus as a fount of
unfathomable mercy for me at the hour of my death, O dying
Jesus, Hostage of mercy, avert the Divine wrath at the hour of
my death. (Diary, 813)

# The Coming of the Lord

*I* do not know, O Lord, at what hour You will come,
And so I keep constant watch and listen
As Your chosen bride,
Knowing that You like to come unexpected,
Yet, a pure heart will sense You from afar, O Lord,

I wait for You, Lord, in calm and silence,
With great longing in my heart
And with invincible desire.
I feel that my love for You is changing into fire,
And that it will rise up to heaven like a flame at life's end,
And then all my wishes will be fulfilled.

Come then, at last, my most sweet Lord
And take my thirsting heart
There, to Your home in the lofty regions of heaven,
Where Your eternal life perdures.

Life on this earth is but an agony,
As my heart feels it is created for the heights.
For it the lowlands of this life hold no interest,
For my homeland is in heaven---this I firmly believe.
(Diary, 1589)

# The Holy Trinity

*O* Holy Trinity, in whom is contained the inner life of God,
the Father, the Son, and the Holy Spirit, eternal joy,
inconceivable depth of love, poured out upon all creatures and
constituting their happiness, honor and glory be to Your holy
name forever and ever.  Amen.  (Diary 525)

# Jesus in the Eucharist

*O*Jesus, concealed in the Blessed Sacrament of the Altar, my only love and mercy, I commend to You all the needs of my body and soul. You can help me, because You are Mercy itself. In You lies all my hope. (Diary, 1751)

*I*bow down before You, O Bread of Angels,
With deep faith, hope and love
And from the depths of my soul I worship You,
Though I am but nothingness.

I bow down before You, O hidden God
And love You with all my heart.
The veils of mystery hinder me not at all;
I love You as do Your chosen ones in heaven
I bow down before You, O Lamb of God
Who take away the sins of my soul,

Whom I receive into my heart each morn,
You are my saving help. (Diary, 1324)

# Prayers During the Hour of Mercy

*O*Blood and Water, which gushed forth from the Heart of Jesus as a fount of Mercy for us, I trust in You. (Diary, 187)

*Y*ou expired, Jesus, but the source of life gushed forth for souls, and the ocean of mercy opened up for the whole world. O Fount of Life, unfathomable Divine Mercy, envelop the whole world and empty Yourself out upon us. (Diary, 1319)

*Y*ou Yourself, Jesus, purely out of love for us, underwent such a terrible Passion. Your Father's justice would have been propitiated with a single sigh from You, and all Your self-abasement is solely the work of Your mercy and Your inconceivable love…At the moment of Your death on the Cross, You bestowed upon us eternal life; allowing Your most holy side to be opened, You opened an inexhaustible spring of mercy for us, giving us Your dearest possession, the Blood and Water from Your Heart. Such is the omnipotence of Your mercy. From it all grace flows to us. (Diary, 1747)

## *Help Me to Be Merciful*

*H*elp me, O Lord, that my eyes may be merciful, so that I may never suspect or judge from appearances, but look for what is beautiful in my neighbors' souls and come to their rescue.

Help me, that my ears may be merciful, so that I may give heed to my neighbors' needs and not be indifferent to their pains and moanings.

Help me, O Lord, that my tongue may be merciful, so that I should never speak negatively of my neighbor, but have a word of comfort and forgiveness for all.

Help me, O Lord, that my hands may be merciful and filled with good deeds, so that I may do only good to my neighbors and take upon myself the more difficult and toilsome tasks.

Help me, that my feet may be merciful, so that I may hurry to assist my neighbor, overcoming my own fatigue and weariness. My true rest is in the service of my neighbor.

Help me, O Lord, that my heart may be merciful so that
I myself may feel all the sufferings of my neighbor. I will
refuse my heart to no one. I will be sincere even with those
who, I know, will abuse my kindness. And I will lock myself up
in the most merciful Heart of Jesus. I will bear my own
suffering in silence. May Your mercy, O Lord, rest upon me.
(Diary, 163)

*E* ternal God, in whom mercy is endless and the treasury of
compassion inexhaustible, look kindly upon us and increase Your
mercy in us, that in difficult moments we might not despair nor
become despondent, but with great confidence submit ourselves
to Your holy will, which is Love and Mercy itself. (Diary, 950)

# The Mysteries of the Rosary

## Joyful Mysteries
- The Annunciation (Luke 1: 26-38)
- The Visitation (Luke 1: 39-56)
- The Birth of Our Lord (Luke 2: 1-21)
- The Presentation of Our Lord (Luke 2: 22-38)
- The Finding of Our Lord in the Temple (Luke 2: 41-52)

## The Luminous Mysteries
- The Baptism of Our Lord (Matthew 3: 13-16)
- The Wedding at Cana (John 2: 1-11)
- The Proclamation of the Kingdom of God (Mark 1: 14-15)
- The Transfiguration of Our Lord (Matthew 17: 1-8)
- The Last Supper (Matthew 26)

## The Sorrowful Mysteries
- The Agony in the Garden (Matthew 26: 36-56)
- The Scourging at the Pillar (Matthew 27: 26)
- The Crowning With Thorns (Matthew 27: 27-31)
- The Carrying of the Cross (Matthew 27: 32)
- The Crucifixion of Our Lord (Matthew 27: 33-56)

## The Glorious Mysteries
- The Resurrection of Our Lord (John 20: 1-29)
- The Ascension of Our Lord (Luke 24: 36-53)
- The Descent of the Holy Spirit (Acts 2: 1-41)
- The Assumption of Mary Into Heaven
- The Coronation of Mary as Queen of Heaven and Earth

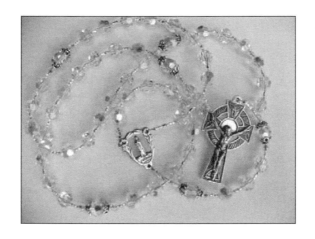

# How to Pray the Rosary

Start by making the Sign of the Cross:
In the name of the Father, and of the Son, and of the Holy
Spirit. Amen.

On the Crucifix on your rosary, pray the I Believe in God...

On the first single bead pray the Our Father...

On each of the next three beads pray the Hail Mary...

On the next single bead, begin by announcing and meditating on
the first mystery and say the Our Father...

On each of the next ten beads pray the Hail Mary...

After the last Hail Mary, pray the Glory be to the Father...

After each decade, pray: O my Jesus, forgive us our sins, save us
from the fires of hell; lead all souls to Heaven, especially those
who are in most need of Thy mercy.

Continue around the rosary until you have completed all five
decades.

# *End with:*

Hail Holy Queen, mother of mercy, our life, our sweetness, and our hope. To thee do we cry, poor banished children of Eve. To thee do we send up our sighs, mourning and weeping in the vale of tears. Turn then, most gracious advocate, thine eyes of mercy toward us. And after this, our exile, show unto us the blessed fruit of thy womb, Jesus. O clement, O loving, O sweet Virgin Mary. Pray for us O holy Mother of God, that we may be made worthy of the promises of Christ. Amen.

O God, whose only begotten Son, by His life, death and resurrection, has purchased for us the rewards of eternal life; grant, we beseech Thee, that by meditating upon these mysteries of the Most Holy Rosary of the Blessed Virgin Mary, we may imitate what they contain and obtain what they promise, through the same Christ our Lord. Amen.

For information on

where you can obtain

additional copies of

<u>Open My Eyes</u>

Visit our website at:

<u>TreasuresofGraceLLC.com</u>

# In Loving Memory of ...

Mary Louise Liberatore

Irene Siedlikowski

Marie Nowadly

*Faithful servants and apostles of God's Mercy*

## St. Maria Faustina Kowalska
### 1905-1938

*And so, my King, I do not ask you for anything,*
*although I know that You can give me everything.*
*I ask You for one thing only;*
*remain forever the King of my heart;*
*that is enough for me.*

~Diary of St. Faustina, 1811~